SUNFLOWER
SHIN SPLINTS

~Siobhan Darling

ISBN: 979-8-9986460-1-0

Printed in the United States of America

Siobhan Darling
www.siobhandarling.com

Dedication

- - - - X

This is to prove that I can.
~To my biggest critic, me.

Content Warning

This book cuts and it's not just the paper.

This collection is a culmination of poetry and prose all centering around relationships and healing. There are topics discussed in these pages that are sensitive in nature. Topics include sexual assault, domestic violence, childhood trauma, homophobia, abuse, child abuse, dissociation, abortion, self-harm, and suicidal ideation. Living through the events that inspired these pieces was not for the faint of heart and I would hope that some of that has been transferred to the page. Please take caution with your own heart and mind.

Names and identifying details have been changed to protect the privacy of individuals.

If you are related to me, for the love of God, do not read this book.

Acknowledgements

First and foremost, I must thank my best friend and editor, Becca, without whom this book would not exist. Your encouragement has and will always be invaluable. Thank you for your time, attention, and handholding as I trudged through this and all the other adventures. I also need to thank my three incredible children, whose very existence and light have guided me through some of the most grueling moments of my life. I live for you my darlings and hope that I can grant you a fraction of the pride you afford me daily. To my brother Sean, who has always supported and taken care of me when I needed him the most. And to my Moonbear, thank you for everything.

Observers may say that I've had a difficult life full of beautifully destructive wildfires. Some may even realize that the arsonist was usually me. Truth is, I've always been one to grow from pain —and for someone so short, I've grown so much. Every growth spurt has brought me closer to the sun.

I wonder if sunflowers have shin splints. Thank the universe for the pain and stretch skyward.

Create shade for those that hurt you. Be the great willow that makes your inner child continue to believe in magic. If you are willing to look, you will find purpose in these existential germinations. They will carve out the most evolved you that has yet to exist. Try not to fall deeply in love with the most recent version of yourself, for she will soon be replaced by the next. I do encourage you to adore her, however. Appreciate her for every blemish she has collected; they will heal, and if tended to properly, the callous will ensure

SUNFLOWER SHIN SPLINTS

that the same fall repeated won't hurt as
greatly. Acknowledge your pain, prioritize your
healing, and grow towards the light.

Mask \'mask\ *n.*

1. a cover or partial cover for the face used for disguise: for the acceptance of polite society when the truth is too unpalatable, too abnormal, too honest. **1.**
(b) a grotesque false face worn at carnivals or in rituals, as in the ritual of passerby lying, the predetermined status of *I'm fine* **2.** a protective covering for the face, resting bitch face affixed to ensure safe passage beneath flickering dim streetlights. *verb.* **1.** to hide or conceal: such as the meticulously painted upturned smile lacquered in cherry red to cover the tear-strewn depression underneath. / The intrinsically groomed behavior, where truth is unkept, / more important to keep others comfortable than risk the potential banishment that comes with becoming transparently authentic. / This mold has been crafted, generationally curated for conformability, but the satin ribbon can't seem to remain tied on the back of my head.
/ As I watch it fall and shatter on the ground there is no fear, no shame, no reflex to hide. / The breeze on my cheek feels of freedom.

My Responsibility

What is my responsibility when it comes to my own trauma? This question has lived inside my soul since the age of seven, following my first violation. Just beginning to explore the world and a singular event stripped me of all security and broke me, like a glass doll and its first of many collisions with the floor, shattered. Broken into weaponized shards, too sharp for soft, caring hands to touch. The start of a heartbreaking cycle, meeting the same villain in different bodies, one break after another. Leaving me even sharper until only abusers are willing to risk the cuts. What then is my fault?

Saying that the answer to this question has evolved over time is not only an understatement, but also disrespectful of the growth achieved. You see, my spiritual path requires a continual exploration of self-honesty, as well as constant self-appraisal. The purpose of these is to be rid of all that stands in the way of altruistic growth and requires respectful reflection, not only on the stained past, but on the non-linear healing rise to the present. Previously I believed that the only way to accomplish this was to find my fault in all behaviors and events of my past. In many cases, I still believe that to be true, after all, without accurate assessment how can we correct?

However, this is no longer my belief when it pertains to trauma. Nor does it pertain to the trauma response behavior cycle I have lived in for most of my life. I need not seek forgiveness for how I survived abuse, I need only to seek healing.

When I started my journey, I blamed myself for my assaults. I won't sugar coat it; I thought I was majorly at fault for being molested and raped. I look back at that girl now with sorrow and compassion for she genuinely thought, "I put myself in dangerous situations and the expected result occurred." What does it say about our society that those assaulted conceive that rape is an event to expect? Thinking back to that mental space brings the taste of cold copper to my tongue; wrong, bitter, and biting. That's the elusive quirk about self-delusion though, isn't it? The sufferer has no conception as to the severity of their own misunderstanding.

That was the case with me, I didn't know what I didn't know.

Though I'm grateful for that stretch of growth, for now, I find myself uniquely qualified to bear witness to those at the beginning of their own journey. A fellow human who has also spent time falsely believing herself to blame for her own misfortune. As time progressed and layers of delusion and misconception fell away, I began to believe that I held a more minor role in my trauma. The self-hatred began to smooth to a place like the slate bedrock of a well-worn creek. That is to say that it was a functional pain. Relatively safe to walk across, cautiously. I thought that a grievous contributor was my inability to say no or to even know that I could. That reasoning took root and held for years. At this place, I believed that if only she could have possessed more self-worth, maybe she could have avoided so much torment.

Though, held up to light —much like the x-ray of a broken wrist— reveals the fracture and fault lines in this thought pattern. A seven-year-old is not responsible for knowing her own "self-worth." And how can anyone expect an innocent child raised in sheltered misunderstanding to know when to say no? This revealing light of self-forgiveness and understanding drove away the last shadowed remnants of blame.

Stripped bare like recently sanded wood, my conceptions have also become softer, gentler, and more useful. This latest plateau has brought me to a place of acceptance— acceptance of self as well as appreciation, for the path I have trudged. Today I believe that I am not at fault for any of my assaults. Today I believe that my only responsibility is to not harm anyone with the shards I grew from surviving my abuse. By recognizing my pain, I continue to heal and soften the remnants of protection that are/ no longer needed.

If shit jobs are miracle grow for dreams, then shit relationships are miracle grow for self-love.

Take Him Out Back

Submissively tracing his steps into the kitchen, conserving the only strength that remains to maintain the level tone of my heightened voice. The tightrope of ensuring that I am loud enough to be heard without appearing angry, lest I trigger an unwelcome reaction.

"Mark, this is serious!" I almost yell to be heard over the thunder of three small children in the cramped living room down the hall, not that volume is never the issue with his ability to hear me. "This is the fourth time this month I've been contacted by the principal regarding his disruptive behavior issues." My throat growing hoarse due to the combination of exasperation of the chase and the continual climb in amplification needed to break through the dull roar emanating from down the hall. "He needs help. I need help! This is your son, what do you want to do about this!?"

He falters to an exaggerated halt at the bottleneck of the hallway, instantaneously spins on his heel, just as the Air Force taught him and barks, spit landing on my chin, "You want to know what I want to do with him?! I want to take him out back and be done with it!"

The ice block in my throat won't budge, but I'm careful not to switch feet, not to lean away from the verbal onslaught. Showing fear has never garnered anything but further force when his eyes take on that glaze. My every hair stands at attention as I take in all surrounding information, the whiskers of my self- protection system. Pupils widen as adrenaline pulses through my quickened heart.

In that moment I see him, just behind the raised collarbone of my enraged husband-turned-assailant, his oldest son, Billy. The fear in his eyes mirror mine to the point of excruciating pain. This isn't the first time Mark has threatened that sweet, tortured boy's life, but this is the first time Billy has been in earshot. This particular intimidation tactic is usually reserved for just me -a muzzle, a harsh reminder that I can't leave him, not if I want to protect that boy. The boy that's been mine since he had just turned three. My oldest, my child that was born of my heart rather than my uterus. The child that is mine in all ways except on paper.

This was never supposed to happen. I was too smart to be a beaten wife, too strong to be held beneath constant fear, too empowered to succumb to a life as this. There is literature on what entails an abusive marriage, endless questionnaires to see if you're in one, and even well-meaning explanations on *Why He Acts This Way*. What of the lead up, though? What of the unfamiliar path to toxicity? They never discuss how you get from honeymoon to backhand. There isn't enough illustration of the grooming. The dreadfully slow transformation from charming to captor.

Keeping the doting husband's costume in their pocket, for special occasions, only for others. The facade thuds to the floor the moment the deadbolt on the front door locks out curious eyes.

In the deepest moments of my Stepford wife hell, I saw a poster taped to the pale blue wall of a gynecologist's bathroom that read, "Domestic violence isn't an anger management issue, abusers have no problem managing their anger when there are witnesses." I used to daydream about what it would have been like if I had followed the directions given by the poster's caption and told one of those caring women of my wedding ring turned shackle. I memorized the emboldened toll-free number since I couldn't risk saving it to my phone. I turned the shape of those numbers on my tongue into a mantra to get through the worst nights. I kept it as my own personal ejection button, which I reserved for whenever his abuse finally crossed the line in the sand that I kept erasing and moving to keep up with his ever-worsening behavior.

Did you know that on average it takes an abused spouse seven attempts before they commit to leaving? I can't name how many times I packed up the kids while they slept during the safety of his night shift just to unpack again before daybreak. There was this distinct insanity that suffocated me during my abuse. As the years passed all the shine and willpower began to drain away. I imagine that is exactly how the grooming is meant to work. It's like boiling a frog, the temperature rises one degree at a time, so slowly that you acclimate to the new homeostasis. The victim doesn't jump out of the scalding pot because, "It's not that bad." And there are many who never jump out of the pot at all. Though the most terrifying reality of grooming is that the process took away all my outside support. Years of meticulously manipulating everyone in my circle. When I finally had the hope necessary to leave, I lost much more than my abuser.

Years later my gut still turns when old acquaintances drone the familiar cliche, "Really? I always thought he was such a nice guy."

So did I bud, that's kinda the whole damn point.

Grief is a Denser Emotion Than Love.

The Kavanaugh Trials

The weathered wood of the picket side gate threatens splinters as I gingerly pull it closed behind me. A new layer of maple and oak leaves hush the sound of gravel under each step. I reorganize my handfuls of coffee, purse, and keys in time to reach the kitchen door. The beauty of working for a small home-based agency is the informality of it all. I call out morning pleasantries, to no reply. Breaching the living room doorway, I realize my married couple bosses, and only two co-workers, are stationed firmly on the couch, squarely focused on the C-SPAN broadcast.

"What's this?" I question.

"Dr. Ford is testifying against Trump's Supreme Court nominee," Robby replies.

Jill interjects prompted by the question across my brow, "You must have heard! Kavanaugh has been accused of assault. Makes sense that Trump's pick would be scum!"

"We will be in the office in just a moment, but we'll make sure to turn up the volume for you," Robby assures.

Though I smiled politely at the assurance, the thought of listening to this soft-spoken woman reliving her worst night brought an immediate dryness to my mouth.
The hardwood creaks at the entrance to the sunroom turned home office. Settling into my corner desk, routine sets in and guides my body through turning on and logging into my computer. I begin combing through emails to gain my bearings on the day's work. As promised, the television volume rises in time to hear the drone of some unseen man monologue about the necessity of timekeeping during the hearing. The import of his colleagues restraining themselves to their respective five minutes of questioning.
Diving deeper into my list of venue contracts in need of signatures, I attempt to occupy as much of my focus as I could on monotony.

The disembodied voice of an unknown, aged politician breaks my concentration,

"You were quite clear that it was Brett Kavanaugh who covered your mouth to prevent you from screaming and then you escaped. How are you so sure that it was him?" she coldly interrogated.

The question and its delivery hardened the back of my throat. As Dr. Blasey Ford eloquently explains how the neurotransmitters encode trauma memories into the hippocampus, I silently struggle to find breath. Without permission or warning, intrusive thoughts envelop my mind. The weight of his clumsy hand, his fingertips finding their grip in the hollow of my cheeks, the overwhelming stench of cheap whisky billowing off his every word.

Can You Go Back Home Again?

I want to take a moment and take a snapshot of my life currently, mostly because I am in awe of it honestly.

In June, I realized that I had exhausted all my options in North Carolina. This beautiful dream peddled on the passionate tongue of that gorgeous woman had fully crumbled. The infatuation had crushed me, mind, body, and spirit. I turned away from the compass of motherhood, the guiding light that prioritizing my children had always been. Choosing an unstable, fiery goddess above them. What a wound that self-awareness created; it was remarkable there was anything left of me. I felt like cult followers once the Kool-Aid wears off, the upside-down bloated frog in a rolling boil. How could I allow myself to fall so far? How could I have been so foolish to trust my own codependent self-sufficiency? Why would I wander into the darkness knowing full well what the sun's warmth could do for the soul?

The only viable path was paralyzing, accepting help from one of the purest souls I have ever had the pleasure of knowing.

SUNFLOWER SHIN SPLINTS

Oliver Everett Cooper has been terrifying me for almost 10 years. My imposter syndrome screamed at the depth of his care; my nonexistent self-esteem cringed at his perspective of my internal beauty. I, responding to secure commitment in the manner feral cats view new humans, ran at the first sign of stability every time. The agreement was set, he would supply the sheltered raised bed for the severed cuttings of my fragile sanity, and I would provide benign chaos and novelty to the stark walls of his newly finished three bed, two bath reno. An unbalanced trade in my view, but I am not one to inspect the mouths of prized horses.

The Volvo full, two kids, one cat, one hound, and a paper bag of mixtapes, we headed south. Moving "home" is not something I wanted to do. Brevard County is a vortex for locals, you can't logic your way out, and once escaped, it has a way of dragging you back. As far as hometowns go, this one is small, conservative, stifling. I never quite fit. As the humidity percentage rose, surprisingly so did the feeling of hope. How unfamiliar that one-time companion now felt.

SUNFLOWER SHIN SPLINTS

There's something about my mental illness
quirks; hope is the foundation on which every
single one of my good days takes root. Not
unlike a backyard garden, it requires constant
care. For two years I gave every ounce of my
care and attention to that woman, the flame of
our entwined passion. That seems to be the
thing with passion in my experience, it's a
flame.
Much like its real-life counterpart, it can
become uncontrollable destruction with nothing
more than a stiff breeze. I have always been so
infatuated with the feeling of falling in love.
The intoxication of being all consumed by
something so ethereal and intangible. You would
think after being burned so deeply I would
recoil at the first sensation of simmer.

Perhaps that's how Oliver snuck back in,
between the still-opened cracks from my fall.
His touch, his love, wasn't the exhilarating
bite of a loose ember, it wasn't the shock of
heat against your face when a doused bonfire
erupts at first light. He was warmth, slow,
inviting, and gentle. Like pulling your arms
into an oversized sweater, sipping spiced chai
snuggled up on the couch. Unlike the dazzling
and unpredictable allure of

dancing fire, this was a way of promised healing. His love came with no expectations nor limits. Like many before him, he was attracted to my light. His very own personal sunshine, but unlike others he showed no desire to hoard it, merely to tend, nurture, and bask in its brilliance.

So, where's the catch? Where's the can of green paint, still dripping from covering the flags? How could this be true, how could you possibly be this kind, selfless, gracious? I did what I could to scare him off, again, including but not limited to:

Multiple debilitating panic attacks, slight break of reality (not needing hospitalization), polyamory, trauma responses mid-coitus, insistence of self- sufficiency (without necessary means), "one-woman-warrior," radio silence, emotional blackouts, tectonic mood shifts, etc.

Run he did not. He reassured me and did his best to reconnect with me. Helpfulness seemed to be his only motive. Genuine care doesn't feel like reckless passion, it feels like a stray getting comfortable enough to fall asleep at your side. It feels like safety, it feels like home.

Even still, fear plagued me, convinced that his acceptance was conditional, for that's all I've ever known. So innately, love has always been synonymous with conditions and conformity. Be this version of yourself to be loved. Quiet that part of you to gain acceptance and adoration. And it's not like I hadn't tried, broke my back to become lovable. And every time, it failed, and I was no blameless bystander. The hurt caused was the consequence of living fraudulently, unintentionally, or otherwise. So, when I rediscovered I was poly, I wasn't about to make that mistake again. Though there was this nagging doubt that the only part of Oliver that was in true agreement was his codependency. That non-monogamy was the inconvenience of being with me.

At every spiral he was patient compassion, a respite of reassurance from the cruelties of my own mind. I had never experienced such acceptance, the feeling of being not only seen but appreciated for all the things about myself that I had been told were wrong or broken. As a direct result of this, I flourished as I never knew possible. My soul bloomed with the freedom of wildflowers reclaiming a field. I rediscovered writing as I learned more about myself, I began to feel at home in my own skin. More than that, as I learned, I began to love, to cherish this woman, all her scars and all her strength. I think that's what a healthy relationship should be, growthful, mutually beneficial and concluding precisely when it's supposed to.

I'm much like Florida, beautiful and at moments serene, slightly trashy, and chock full of shit that could kill.

Home

On our third date she told me that I felt like
home,
And that scared her.

She may have been the first to speak it, But I
certainly understood the feeling.

When I hold her,
She feels how I've always hoped home would
feel like.

When I settle into her neck,
She smells like chicken noodle soup.

When she wraps her arms around me,
She feels like that hand-crocheted blanket my
mother never had the time to make.

When she kisses me,
She feels like sanctuary.

Her lips -the curtain to the closet hideaway I
made as a child.
Everything stands still.

Everything from the outside is shut out.

SUNFLOWER SHIN SPLINTS

All the noises stop, Even in
my head.

That's how I knew.
The first time she kissed me, My
brain grew quiet.

I've never had that happen, Well,
not sober.

I feel like when you find someone that gets your
brain to silence.

That,
That is home.

Dandelion

Like a late spring dandelion's second
bloom,
Already bright and glinting in the sun, Blossoms
into a thousand wish-filled plume, And with that
same speed, my fall had begun.

I nurtured you as you became planted, Promise of
freshly tilled earth; what could be,
How could I have known the soil was tainted,
Enraptured, velvet lies all I could see.

Obsession weeds invade the garden beds,
Symbiotic growth veers parasitic, Sprouts
wilt as the noxious deception spreads,
I choke as you grow more narcissistic.

To rid the poison, I must scorch the field,
Survival seems like death before it's healed.

~Codependency

My Heart Breaks Only for You

I've never known a love that didn't bring
as much pain as it did pleasure and I loved you
more than anything. You made my soul so happy,
and we had a great life, but I let the darkness
inside me convince me otherwise. Sometimes all I
wanted to do was run away from you to prove to
you I'm important and special, but I was
paralyzed by the thought that you wouldn't care
enough to search for me. I was stuck in place
thinking that any void I left would have been so
easily filled. What if I am not a prize worth
fighting for? So, I stayed, panic stricken,
striving to just be enough to keep you from
walking away first.

You could sense this, my insecurities.
I made you feel like you weren't enough, that
your love wasn't enough to quiet my demons. I
tried to show you that it wasn't your
responsibility, that I loved how much you loved
me. I worked on my flaws and grew to love
myself, but in turn it became a mirror to your
own feelings of insufficiency. In turn you
couldn't love yourself enough to believe someone
else loved you. So, you left, but oh how I loved
you. Oh, how I believed and even still do

that our world together was magic, that could have lasted a lifetime.

Want to know what a bullet to the heart feels like? It feels like the love of your life calling you by your legal name.
Seems innocent enough, but not when to them you are babe, baby, sweetheart, love.
Anything, but your name. Then they pierce your heart with that familiar combination of sounds, instantly transforming you back to what you were before you were theirs.

There is nothing quite like the moment you get your heart broken to make you so aware of the functions of your body. You lose all attachment to the world around you, all you can do is focus on the feeling of your internal systems trying to keep you alive. It's the solitary reminder that time, undeterred, persists even amidst the illusion of a halted world. Isn't it interesting that time suspends for both the inception of love, as well as its finale?
Your heartbeat so present you feel your pulse in your ears. Your eyes burn as they fight back the urge to drown your cheeks with your pain. Your stomach pushes at you trying to turn the sadness into a physical entity that it can expel from your being. Anything your body can do to make the pain go away. It's trying to regain homeostasis,

but your mind is incapable of fulfilling that plan.

Try as it might, nothing happens. Nothing makes it go away. Not crying, not laughing, not sleeping, not eating. It distracts, but the pain sits. It lasts and lasts. It's a lump in your throat, a churn in your belly, an ache in your chest, that stays with you for so long that it becomes your new self. You stop noticing it after a while. You begin to think you have finally passed it, but it's just the way your body now sits at rest, like a dull ringing in your ears or the ticking of a clock hand, still present, but you block it out. When you do realize it's still there it's blaring. It takes everything you are to push it down again. It's not until your heart finds something else to beat for, that you notice the pain lift and your lungs experience a full breath of air as if for the first time.

I hope one day I find someone who will love me the way that I love you and I pray with everything in me that when that day comes, I will be able to love them back. Although every fiber of my being wants it to only be you.

Until then, my love, my heart breaks only for you.

Dear Father,

I have spent most of my life trying to convince myself that I don't require your approval to validate my existence; I mentally orphaned myself 18 years ago. It was less painful than continuing to wait for a father that could not, would not step up. All I wanted was a father to be proud of. To be a daughter you couldn't help but show up for. And time after time I needed you and you weren't there. I stopped waiting. I stopped having expectations for you to fall short of. I stripped you of that unearned title. I chose no father over an incapable one. Though it left such a large wound, I figured it was best to move towards healing than constantly dressing new gashes.

Then the unimaginable happened. God lifted you out of your self-imposed prison and carried you until you could stand on your own. Little by slowly, I was introduced to a man I had never met. He was clear-eyed and clean-shaven, eloquent, soft-spoken, fiercely intelligent, and hardworking. A beautiful example of a gentleman. Though there was a sense of too little too late. How could any amount of redemption make up for such deep scars? Though you weren't seeking redemption, a piece of you knew that was an impossible task. Instead, you merely put one day in front of another and strived to be a better person today than you were yesterday. I didn't "get my father back," I met and grew to know the man before me, not as a father but as a fellow human.

Though the relationship wasn't an emotionally close one, it was a significant companionship, one at times that I was less than deserving of. It was a working relationship, with boundaries and mostly mutual respect, I was still a kid after all. And now that there was a functional adult present, I was afforded the chance to take off the oversized caregiver uniform and fit into something more age appropriate.

Through many growing pains we fell into some kind of normal routine and that was fine. It was more than I had ever expected, so how could I not be grateful? You were never the mushy type with me, you demonstrate your care through tangible acts of service, shared musical interests, and dark humor. It works for us.

SUNFLOWER SHIN SPLINTS

When the day came that I fell and fell hard, the last person I would have ever imagined came to pick me up, you. With love and compassion, I never knew existed here, between us. I needed a dad and there you were. You showed up, not just for me, but for my babies as well. You effortlessly transformed from an awkward mentor into exactly what I needed, a father. A father that I couldn't be prouder to claim as mine. And somehow, as soon as I no longer required your approval, I had it. I had grown into a daughter you couldn't help but be proud of.

You and I have gone through enough evolution to put Darwin to shame, separately and together. You have been so many things to me, some good, some bad. You have held many roles, father, drunk, ward, stranger, fellow, and mentor, but my absolute favorite so far must be Dad.

We may never have the relationship I dreamt of as a little girl nor the one that I deserve now. I will never get back the childhood that your demons stole from me and most of my healing has been done by my own hands and the hands of the other blameless child, meant to be held by you, not picking up the pieces left in your wake. Though he wasn't made to fill your role and was only a child himself, your son did a beautiful job in your stead.

Despite all of this, I've blossomed into a fiercely self-reliant, wittily sardonic, unexpectedly tender-hearted woman who acknowledges that the only unwavering element in our connection is change, and ideally, personal evolution.

Imperfectly,

Your Daughter

Anthology of Ana

How I hate to watch your eyes as they begin
to well. And the knowledge that my words have
inspired your tears. You ask to know me, but
though I am no longer a prisoner to those scars,
they cut you through. You and your beautiful
soul. That is precisely what I first fell for.
Which is impressive due to the laundry list of
your crush-worthy traits.

Beautiful
Intelligent Kind
Thoughtful Talented
Adorable Authentic
Emotional Depth Tiny
Racoon Hands

Your readiness to expose your heart is
terrifying. Your availability to bear your
joyful essence is magnetic. Watching you dance
with abandon at the show, I can't picture it
without smirking. In that moment no one existed
but you, being enveloped by

the music. A private show for your perfect spirit. Eyes gently closed, contentment softening your already elvish features.

That freeness once lived in my soul; pomp and circumstance dulled that shine. Lovers desperate to cage that spirit finally succeeded. I have no desire to cage your heart, I understand that is no way to keep it. What I want is to be your safe space, your favorite field to graze. A beautiful resting place between your adventures.

I want to show you how perfect your smile is, how your hips are my favorite hills to road trip my fingers down.
Regardless of their destination, the cashmere of you sends anticipatory warmth through my veins.

Broken Carousels

There are days that I genuinely feel too damaged to function. As though the combination of childhood trauma response, cyclical abuse, and codependent behavior patterns will always eventually end in despair and mutual destruction for all parties involved. I didn't choose my family of origin; I didn't choose my cornucopia of mental illnesses or the sexual, physical, and psychological abuses I have endured.
There is, however, this constant thread of wonder revolving around my Complex PTSD. What is my part? How much of the cycle is my involvement? What do I attract by being damaged?

There are so many books regarding the trauma response manifestation of abuse survivors, the generational patterns, and how to spot them. They explain the reason why narcissists are attracted to, and successful at preying on once traumatized people. How do you take this information and apply it to build a successful life full of healing and wholeness? Especially when every forward step feels more like regression than achievement. When instead of triumph, you just keep creating new cycles. New carousels of the exact same choices but with different players and slightly altered storylines. At which point is it better to just admit defeat? At which point is it better to just resign to the idea that you are too far gone to establish significant footing? When do we become a garden left unattended and open to all the disgustingness of human nature? Poisoned by the harshness of salt spray and the constant affront of acid rain. Soil that is so infertile that regrowth won't occur; those new roots, no matter how they are tended to, will never hold steadfast.

Stitch

I don't know how to be less,
I don't know how to be less without
suffocating.

I don't know how to be smaller,
It's not as if I haven't tried,
To fit through that particular needle's eye.

Stitch myself into the perfect size.
Something comfortable — conforming.
Something palatable — confining.

Downsize from crazy to eccentric,
Soften from too much to quirky.

What do you do,
When you find out that being you,
Hurts those you love,

Again
And again
And again?

Teacher Between My Lungs

Barely bandaged from the southern fall, On
the mend with no direction.

How do I find the exit for this carousel
When I can't even stand?

Through the smoke comes a silhouette,
Sweet as iced tea.

Handpicked flowers in a violet vase.
Strong, dexterous fingers whisper across my arm.

The sensation like honeybees,
Every freckle buzzes a light.

You taught me so much,
You taught me how to fall again.
You taught me that passion does not always have
to be destructive.
And how to celebrate how far I have come.
You gave me a nourished flower bed to replant
pieces of my heart that I would rather have just
thrown away.
Without you, I would never be where I am today.

SUNFLOWER SHIN SPLINTS

You taught me how to prioritize myself.
How to stand on boundary lines.
You taught me what bare minimum was and how to
climb my expectations to heights I deserve.
You taught me what signs I had failed to
recognize before.
Your kindness sheltered my way out of the
darkness.
Your fierceness relit my own.
Your mind awoke my slumbering potential.

Your hands reminded me that this body is mine.
Your lips discovered more in one sunlit
afternoon than all the others had before.
Your love made my chest ache from expansion.
But your eyes, your eyes were everything.
The compassion of a shared history, the hopeful
light upon the unknown path ahead, the sparkling
mischief of temptation.

How bitter irony can be. You taught me that
I deserved better than you had to offer. The
fresh breeze that trailed as you walked into my
life grew to storm clouds as your air of
jealousy appeared. For once, red flags did not
go unnoticed.

SUNFLOWER SHIN SPLINTS

You threw the same signals you warned against. I drew boundaries of safety, just like you taught me. Never thinking that they would be needed to guard against you and your affront on my newfound stability. Your arrogant assumptions as to what I needed, mere moments after you taught me that only I could know what that was. So afraid to lose, you lost your standing, fell from my graces as quickly as you helped create them.

The last sensation you left, once the storm withdrew, was that of gratitude.
Teacher between my lungs.

My Favorite Mess

I have a Starbucks drink, not because I love that pretentious dumpster of a coffee shop but because I love you and your beautiful, basic soul.

You are my favorite mess; I will always be up for kneeling down in your chaos and sorting through your latest disaster.

When you're treading water and can't reach my hand in the lifeboat, I will jump in beside you. What I mean to say is you will never be alone again.

Truth is you never were, we just hadn't met. Not truly. It wasn't until I saw your soul on your worst day that I could look back at mine and say, you will be okay. This, just like all the other worst days, will not kill you. You are not wrong, bad, evil.

You are impeccably, exquisitely human.

When Mere Existence Means Confrontation

You will spend way too much of your life hating
yourself;
This is internalized homophobia.

You will be warned not to come out of the closet
For fear of judgment and familial disownment.

When you finally begin to live authentically,
Many of your fears will be proven true.

The hate you receive directly will not hurt
nearly as much
As the hate your children experience by proxy.

You will be told that your queerness is actually
trauma response
So repeatedly that you will often question that
yourself.

Regardless of whether you were born this way or
chose this,
You are valid.

SUNFLOWER SHIN SPLINTS

And how badass is it for someone to fearfully
choose bliss,
In lieu of societal suffocation?

There will be times that you are so tired of
coming out,
That you default to omissive blending.

Take your rest and recharge,
Because there will always be more fights to
weather.

And our battlefield is everywhere
When mere existence means confrontation.

Keep your "family" chosen and
unconditional,
Because love without acceptance isn't love.

One day when you no longer need outside
validation,
You will find yourself surrounded and celebrated
for being,
Imperfectly, Unapologetically, Immaculately You.

Reality is this beautifully broken thing, neither chronological nor logical. Rather, it is the junction place where the past and/or the future intrude, sometimes painfully, on the present moment.

DON'T PANIC.

Descending into a Facebook video hole, I fail to recognize that the pregnancy test has stopped blinking.

"Some bleeding is normal after a surgical abortion and shouldn't be more than a regular period. Take this in four weeks; if it's negative, all clear. No need to call for post-op."

"And if it's positive?"

These new-age tests are so irritating in their ease of use. No space left for question, no margin for debate, no faint lines to comprehend. Emboldened black neutral lettering with a perceived air of arrogance to the left on the otherwise blank gray results window, mere inches away from my urine.

Pregnant

My merciful brain has this loving trauma response where it encases me in an emotion-free bubble when reality is too much.

    I wonder who suggested the font. Do you think there was an adjunct committee appointed? What were their credentials? Advertisement execs with a focus on how well this display option would read on Instagram posts. Or perhaps fertility specialists, with all their combined experience of delivering blissful life- changing announcements as well as heartbreaking tragic realizations? Or maybe there was a demure admin who thought back to the description of the font used on the Hitchhiker's Guide to the Galaxy, "big friendly letters, DON'T PANIC." What exactly makes letters friendly anyhow?
These letters don't appear friendly, I'd prefer "DON'T PANIC." Not that I would be capable of following that specific direction.

~

My back sticking to the same vinyl-covered, obnoxiously loud print-cushioned chair, positioned in the same spot next to the only window that opens. Staring at the same four wallpaper clad hotel walls as every channel blur into the same monotonous background noise.

Wondering if it's too soon to call Sadie again, only to realize it's only been two hours since the last time I called. Backing out of TikTok to scroll through the family album; being on the road is always tough, but this trip is an entirely new level. No distractions, no people, no routine to break up the loneliness. Flipping through the pictures from our summer road trip, the boys gritted smiles in their first day of school pictures, the obligatory family shots on

mom's stairs at Thanksgiving. I stop on a short video of Sadie playing Santa, wearing the sweats I bought her last year, hair still a mess from late night present wrapping. Passing out gifts to all three kids and then sitting on the edge of the couch cushion soaking in every second of the giggling excitement. I'm not sure this level of nostalgia makes me miss them any less or makes this confinement

any more bearable. I'll give it another hour and then send a simple text, see if she's busy.

~

I pop back into my consciousness and return to the present moment, I stand over the otherwise innocuous piece of plastic. What does this mean? Confusion overwhelms all senses. Reality begins to tune out of focus. My hearing begins to wobble, noises of the house become distorted, like listening underwater. My depleted body gently slides my back down the veneered

66

doors of the vanity, slumping onto the tile
as a child would onto their mother's lap. Though
my own arms are the only ones to envelop me. The
sobs are uncontrollable, thoughts flying at
unrecognizable speed. Two desperate questions
land at the forefront. What does this mean? Am I
pregnant again, or still? Spawned from this
thought, anxiety's cruel grasp constricts my
esophagus, ever so slowly, pressure builds until
I'm gasping.

Desperation unlocks the phone; mercy
answers the line.

"Hi Pumpkin Pie, what's good?" a voice
like bottled sunshine.

Attempting to speak around the ice cutting
at the back of my throat, "Lex, it says - but I
don't understand!" gasping.

"Okay, okay, focus on your breath honey,"
she soothes. "I'm so sorry, but I can't hear
you, love."

Closing my eyes, I try to re-enter my body,
attempting to regain control over my lungs. My
racing heart is a lost cause but maybe I can get
a handle on my

hyperventilation before my vision cuts to black.

"It… the follow-up test… it says I'm pregnant. What does that mean? I don't want to go through that again, not alone. I was so sure, I felt so certain! I don't want to do that all over again, not alone!" I plead, unable to blink the tears at bay any longer.

Awareness dampens her tone, "Have you called Ollie?"

"And say what?"

~

I reply with I love you, though there's so much more I wish I could say. She's always been better with words than I am. I'm better with action; give me a crisis, a flat tire, something to fix. Hell, if I could just hold her. Let her tears soak the front of my shirt and then assure her it's not a big deal when she pulls back and tries to apologize.
She's never been allowed to break, never allowed to just break down and feel. She's always been the strong one, always had to take care of everyone else. Raise three kids alone, no wonder she didn't want to go through it again. She's already had two other men leave her with more

mouths to feed, more people for her to care for. All I want is to be there for her, her safe spot where she can finally just be. When she needs me, where am I? On the other side of the continent. When she finally reaches out, what do I say? Nothing.

~

The conversation lasted three minutes and twenty-two seconds. Most of which was weighted silence. He sat there 1,352.5 miles (2,176.63776 km) away, in the middle of mandatory quarantine for a job outside of Toronto. He was searching for anything to say that wasn't, "I'm so sorry I'm not there," since he knows how I despise that line. Though the lack of saying it when we both know he's thinking it might as well have been cerebral screaming.

I shatter the quiet with, "If I'm going to sob into the void, I'd rather do it alone."

"The grocery store refused to deliver my food," he says.

"What?"

"Yeah, they said they don't do that. But the manager at that pizza joint said he would drop me off a short-list. I guess I've made a friend," he continues.

I push the phone to the other side of the pillow so clearing my nostrils goes unnoticed. Voice control returns, briefly.

"I have to change over the boys' laundry," I said.

"Oh, of course."

"I'll call you later, okay?" My voice betrays me on the question.

"Sadie?" he said.

"I'll talk to you later baby, I love you." My finger hovering the disconnect button long enough for his reply.

Wish granted; I scream into the void until the breath is gone.

Thorns

I really wish that during episodes I grew
thorns,
So that everyone around me would know,
Exactly how prickly I would be if they dared
to touch.

Anyone who could get close would know not to
hug,
Not to caress,
Not to even sit near me.

Because I am incapable of not cutting, I
don't mean to, lord knows I don't want to,
And the pain is two-sided and paralyzing.

I would be able to show everyone,
Just how much pain I'm actually in.

Giant thorns ripping up through my skin,
Dripping garnets.

Self-protection at its worst,
Invisible.

Looking this normal,

SUNFLOWER SHIN SPLINTS

While feeling this odd,
Is the worst part of the curse.

The grace of the universe is wonderfully merciful in that way. Just when I need it, there it is. Not to be confused with when I want it or even when I ask for it.

Bare Moon Bliss

The Gaelic language has a phrase, Anam Cara, which translates to soul-friend. It is meant to describe a unique connection that a person is destined to have with someone else. That person could be a friend, companion, or spiritual guide. For me, that person is Becca. She is joy and hope-made human, she is one of those people that can elevate a trip to the gas station from a mere errand to an adventure.

During her last visit from New York, these spontaneous fun-creating skills were at their peak. This whole pandemic put a damper on some of our more favored activities, which mostly revolve around being in large groups of humans. We traded club hopping for nights of binging Netflix and ordering in from all the local restaurants I've hooked her on during past trips. Sun-drenched days spent lounging poolside, chatting about everything from Tinder fails to daydreaming of future travels. No topic is ever off-limits between us, no judgment, just comfort and laughter.

SUNFLOWER SHIN SPLINTS

Ours is a friendship of journey. We have walked hand in hand through more personal victories and tragedies in four years than some people have experienced their entire lives. By far our longest hike has been the continuous trek to find self- acceptance and the even more elusive self- love. Though this summit seems to be a moving target, there is no one I trust more to stand on the firing line of life with me than her. If only she wasn't straight, I'd make her the most blushing bride, but not all of us can be perfect. So instead, I'll just adore her and together we shall grow old, platonically, happily ever after.

I would love to say that our connection was a product of love at first sight, but that wouldn't simply qualify as an exaggeration, it would be an outright lie. During our first meeting, I found Becca to be annoying, too loud, and too joyful. At the time, my internalized self- hatred, and my litany of unmedicated mental illnesses would never allow me to take up the kind of space I was witnessing this woman command. My default back then was a calculated air of withdrawn mystery in all unfamiliar social encounters. Better to dull one's shine in the hopes of blending than risk any potential persecution from the dreaded and impossible task of genuine authenticity. In this pessimistic mind frame, my opinion of Becca was not as severe as an abhorrence, but closer to mild distrust. It wasn't until several gatherings later that I had the blessing of truly seeing her. The night happened to coincide with a particularly awful suicidal ideation episode that I was grinning and bearing through when the woman parted her lips, and my most intimate thoughts began spilling out of her mouth. She was annotating in uncomfortable detail the exact slideshow of horror currently debuting inside my own psychologically marred mind. Here was a real human who intimately knew the darkness that I was trapped in, but she wasn't trapped. She had found an escape hatch; she spoke of found freedom, and it sounded like morning birds. Her story might as well have been that of a Pegasus flight, for it was a path I never thought possible. The possibility of not merely functioning but of thriving despite a life that tried to kill us. I had to have what she had found, and just like that, our destined path began.

SUNFLOWER SHIN SPLINTS

Beginning to fully melt into the overstuffed cushions of the green corduroy sectional nestled into the corner of my darkened living room after a full day of not much in particular, we recount all the movies we already ticked off our watch list. The list we compiled on our road trip down through the mountains of West Virginia, in between her constant inability to take a decent picture of the sunset due to her easily distracted mind and complete lack of patience. It was the magic hour one starts experiencing as they approach their thirties; on the one hand, we could wash our faces, change into sweats, and veg out to yet another episode of *The Office* or we could grab the keys and find some nonsense to get into. That is the exact moment the thought hit me.

"Do you want to go skinny-dip in the ocean?" I questioned, more than half expecting a snorting "NO!" in response. To both of our surprise, she giggled, "Yes!"

As we start driving across the barely lit causeway toward sleepy beachside, Becca grabs my phone and struggles to unlock the device so she can gain control of the night's soundtrack. Frustrated, she haphazardly shoves the phone directly into

my eye line, while I'm driving, in the hopes
that the facial recognition will finally grant
her access to my Spotify account. The phone
unlocks and as she's muttering to herself how
obnoxious iPhones are, she begins to navigate
through my library of alternative indie pop and
spoken word playlists. Harmless annoyance
floating off her heightened shoulders like
ultra- fine glitter. To alleviate some rising
tension, I take the phone and begin to type the
title of a throwback track that we had
reminisced about earlier in the day. Her smile
stretches her cheeks wide as the brass horn
starts playing over the sound system. Somehow,
she remembers every single word, with sound
effects, to Mambo Number
5. The anxiety that had unknowingly tightened my
jaw softens before we make it to the second
refrain. We park the car and, still giggling, we
start traversing the unlit path towards the
boardwalk. I'm explaining to her how it's
currently sea turtle season and for their
protection there are no artificial lights
allowed on the beach as we break through the
wall of overgrown sea oats and realize there's
no need for the flashlight anyway. The moon is
high and just shy of full; the diffused

light is draped over every glinting grain of
sand. It is illuminating every crashing wave,
silhouetting groups of two scattered across the
dunes.

We exchange guesses as to what debauchery
the couple closest to the boardwalk is up to
as we walk past them toward the intrinsic call
of the lapping waves. The sand is still warm
from being bathed in the midsummer heat all
day. The weight of the salty air grounds my
firing nerves. I may come across as a self-
confident force of a woman, but it is a well-
worn mask. Threadbare from constant use, an
intangible relic from a life of survival.

Before my whole mind can run away from me,
we cross a shelf of dried seaweed, a harsh
prickle against bare feet brings the moment back
into focus. We settle on a spot of packed sand
near the mouth of the tide and faster than my
speeding pulse, we strip. Uncontrollable nervous
laughter bubbles up from the deepest parts of my
inner child, signaling mischievous activities to
come. I leave my imaginary protective mask atop
the pile of discarded clothes and run to the
water before my better sense has any chance to
halt me. My

toes relax as the tepid trace of saltwater engulfs my following calf.

That is the exact moment I turn to see Becca, a woman who, despite surviving a life of one hardening experience after another has kept her shimmering open spirit, doubts herself. A woman who doesn't see the exquisiteness of her curves, who habitually hides beneath self-deprecating humor. It's one of the many character traits we share. There she is, baring her soul as well as her body, under possibly the brightest moon I have ever witnessed. Happiness visible in every corner of her face, arms spread to embrace the waves, head thrust upward with laughter. Becca has one of those magical laughs. It is lyrical, catching, and one of the purest sounds; it has this ability to blot out all the nastiness of this world. I can't help but join her, giggling and spinning in the surf.

You can feel the incoming hurricane offshore through the strength of the undercurrent. Pulling at our knees, as though the ocean herself was dancing with us under the playful spotlight of the moon. The feelings of freedom and joy are electric, I can feel them pulsing through

every muscle, sparking out the tips of my fingers as I swipe the crest of the white water with every twirl. There is no space here for doubt, for self-consciousness.
There is no space for anything except unadulterated bliss.

In this perfect moment, it is hard to comprehend what thoughts the ocean used to produce in my younger years. The numerous starlit skies that passed overhead, completely unappreciated. Walking towards the waves alone, wondering how far I could swim before my arms grew too tired to carry my body back to shore. The thought of swimming off into the horizon, leaving all the pain in my wake. I wondered if I would cry as the last morsel of strength was stripped by the undercurrent and the will to tread life was finally removed from me. Would the feeling be one of relief or fear as my lungs filled with water? If only I could tell that girl what was coming, lift her chin, tell her of the love and the joy on the horizon. The beautiful moments that would make all the survival worth it. Even though there will be dark days, someday they will no longer be the norm and will make the light even more brilliant, blindingly so.

SUNFLOWER SHIN SPLINTS

If I could take a snapshot of this moment, these wild, perfect women, would it rightly capture the feeling? Could it possibly do it justice? Or would it be like photographing a harvest moon; still beautiful but nowhere close to the breathtaking magic of real life? I wish I could frame this Becca, this brave magnificent creature. Wrap her in silk and save her for an awful day when everything is rotten and the world gets so small that you can't fully expand your chest. When my soul can feel hers weeping. When both of us need a reminder that this level of perfect moments is possible, but only when we let ourselves live.

SUNFLOWER SHIN SPLINTS

Goosebumps and Butterflies

Sex shouldn't be like that, not the first time.
It goes against the laws of nature.

Touching you for the first time
was like re-reading a favorite novel.

It makes sense that I let you brand me,
You were under my skin from the beginning.

It only seems right that you will haunt my skin,
For the rest of time.

You were always goosebumps and butterflies,
But you can't live like that forever.

Love Scene

You were the first person who ever introduced themselves as a hopeless romantic that I actually believed.

You were as in love with love as I was. And you didn't need to say it.

I could see it, you crafted entire love scenes in your mind, dramatic and ridiculous.

You fancied meet-cutes to the point that you manifested one for us.

You took me on the best dates of my life and I'm not sure if I was ever in love with you. I'm not sure if you were ever in love with me but I know that you and I both loved love so much.

If we had a season, it would be autumn. Cozy, warm, and slow, over far too quickly.

Early nights that last forever.

SUNFLOWER SHIN SPLINTS

Crisp enough to snuggle but not cold enough to
keep you inside.

I think about that a lot.

You were everything I loved about fictional
love. And I got to experience that in real life.

That is a hard thing to recover from.

That's why I need to remind myself. I don't
think you were ever in love with me. And I don't
think I was ever in love with you.

I think we were both unabashedly, entirely, obsessively
in love with love.

And your character description matched my
script.

I cannot convince you to love me as I am.
I have a difficult enough time loving
myself.

Possession

Love doesn't cause difficulty, only
possession does.
Can you truly call it love if all you want to do
is possess it?

My heart is not some fragile object to be kept
and admired, fear gripping fingers harder.
If you treat me as such, this will shatter,
and the fault will be no one's but yours.

What you speak of isn't love, it is
control.
I am something to be adored, not admired.

I am not art, a painting or a sculpture. Some
stagnant creation to be inspected and held.

I am a living, breathing heart-beating force of
nature.
Something to experience with wonder, something
to behold with respect.

Tell Me More

You tell me there's no need,
As I arise from dinner,

To grab you a water,

And then a napkin,
And then parmesan cheese.

You hate that I won't let you help,
As hard as you might try,

To make the food,
Or clear the table,
Or carry the three dishes balanced on my two
arms.

You must understand, I dote because that's
all I can do while remaining appropriate. And
please believe that remaining appropriate with
you is no passive task. It requires every wisp
of faith and daily meditation to remind me that
my plans will always pale in comparison to the
universe. That you are too important to rush.
Because the truth is, all I want to do is scoot
closer, offer my straw as I extend my water to
you. Use the red sauce in the corner of your
mouth as an excuse to trace the line of your jaw

with the blade of my finger. Feed you my own
pasta, to watch your lips caress the fork with
each bite. Staring at your hair, desperate to
know how soft it would feel against my cheek.
Lightly tracing the top of my own thigh to
ensure my hand wouldn't reach across the
neutral zone without my permission.

You excuse yourself outback for an after-
meal smoke and I say I'll join, just to keep you
company, in a calculated, aloof manner. Though
all I'm thinking is how much closer the patio
chairs would place us compared to the separate
couches in the living room. All I can think is
how the ember of your cigarette is the perfect
excuse to stare at your mouth and contemplate
how soft your lips are.
Sitting across the PVC table poolside as the
sunset paints the sky with all her best hues.
The shadows slow-dancing across your face until
the only light remaining is emanating from those
eyes. Even in the dark your smile shimmers, a
luminescence that rivals the moonlight. Turns
the task of making you laugh into the most
gratifying, light-giving challenge. Hours glide
past like minutes, as effortless as the
conversation.

"I have a question," she said, eyes sparkling.

"Oh, god. What?" I retort.

"The other night you asked, why you. So, why me?" she questions.

Leaning back in my lawn chair, gazing at the stars, I inhale slowly.

"No! Don't try and craft the perfect wording. I finally got you vulnerable, don't you dare regress on me," she orders, coy laughter wrapping around every word.

"I'm considering whether or not I'm going to answer," I said.

For if I were to answer honestly it would start with that smirk you flashed the first time I met everyone out for pool. The sound of my name on your tongue as you teased how much you'd love to witness me in a mood. The fact that it's been too long since I've had a chance to verbally spar with anyone of your caliber. The way you watched the whole room without missing a shot. The way you looked up from your cue aimed directly at me without changing intensity levels. I left that night knowing I was in trouble. I've never been one for first-sight falls, I require substance to intrigue my attention, and you have substance for days. You like to say that you're not that deep, you say a lot to invalidate your own significance. However, I've yet to meet an artist with a shallow soul and in yours, I could swim for years, never reaching the bottom. The more facets I see of you, the spark of interest grows.

Every time I hear you speak or watch you help people; it is the perfect combination of compassion and sarcasm. The fact that you're actively working on yourself, pushing yourself even further out of your comfort zone. Your refusal to accept fine.

You are completely terrifying, in the most perfect, immaculate way. You are an inverted loop on a wooden roller coaster that I can't wait to ride. Getting closer to you, getting to know you, learning what thoughts exist behind the sparkle in your eyes. Learning the backstory of every scar. Decoding the intricacies behind the varied subtle differences in your pondering noises and the way that you say, "...Nothing," when you're too afraid or bashful to tell me what you're thinking.

You speak about your progress and growth; shit might as well be porn. Tell me more about therapy, tell me more about stepping up as a mother and co-parenting, tell me more about embracing your pain and healing long scarred wounds.

Please,
Tell
Me
More.

I've been in love with love as long as I can remember.

The Experience of Being Seen

Presenting myself with abandon,
Completely vulnerable to another,
Being appreciated for exactly who I am.

Spent most of my life a chameleon,
Playing the role I thought the world wanted,
Never knowing who I was underneath all those
masks.

As a result, I wasn't creating a lot of
genuine connections.
To attract genuine connections,
I must present a genuine me.

How do I accomplish this if I have no idea who I
am?

A former lover gave me this wonderful phrase,
MasterDate,
It's cheeky and sounds naughty.

Get to know who you are,
What makes you, you.

SUNFLOWER SHIN SPLINTS

So that you can present a genuine you to the
world.

MasterDate myself,
Invest in my longest running relationship. Learn
what I like,
What I don't,
What makes me happy,
What makes me laugh.

With this newfound knowledge, I
have a chance,
To forge authentic connections,
When I present a genuine me.

Refusing Reality

Come away with me,
To the place my heart meets yours,
Clandestinely,
Nightly.

A place where only we exist,
No trauma,
No time constraints.

Only two lovers,
Dancing beneath a starry sky,
Burning wildly,
Unbridled, untamed.

Come away with me, After
bedtime,
When the world is quiet,
Replete with possibility.

Each night I lie here,
Pondering, scheming, wishing.

Rolling the idea of you Over
in my mind,
Until it's as velvet as your cheek.

SUNFLOWER SHIN SPLINTS

Imagining your body pressed to mine,
Refusing reality,
Barely breathing,
Barely daring to believe,
That you might come away with me.

What Every Homeless Junkie Teenage Mom- To-Be Should Know

There is no right or wrong answer to the
question, "Should I have this baby?"
There is only the answer you can live with.

Depending on your state, you may be too far
along to abort by the time you reach the age of
consent.

Regardless of how undevout your divorced,
Catholic parents are, chances are neither of
them will sign consent paperwork.

Sleep deprivation doesn't start with infancy,
but somewhere around the time you can no longer
tie your own shoes.

That no matter your age, when you are preparing
to have a baby, you are no longer a kid.

If you decide to birth and keep this child, know
that statistically, it is likely you will walk
this path alone.

SUNFLOWER SHIN SPLINTS

And that no matter how hard you work and how much you love, you may never fill a dad-sized hole in your child's heart.

That at times you will hold them and wipe their tears as you witness them aggravate the same daddy issues you are all too familiar with.

That there is no such thing as being financially ready to have a baby.

And not to worry about giving your child all the stuff you didn't have growing up but concern yourself with being the person you didn't have.

Know that everyone screws up their kids, as will you, but don't stress that you're doing that trauma inducing, therapy-needed thing *right now*.

Remember that having good parents isn't a prerequisite for being one.

There truly is nothing more healing for childhood trauma than being a compassionate, present parent.

SUNFLOWER SHIN SPLINTS

Regardless of how many hopes and dreams you have for your kid, when they begin to tell you who they are, just listen.

For you didn't give birth to a houseplant or some inanimate doll, you gave birth to a completely autonomous human being.

And your only real job is to keep them alive and help shape and guide them to being healthy, happy, and self-sufficient people.

This path will take so much from you, your youth, your freedom, your ability to jump on a trampoline and not pee a little.

What it will give you; the rare privilege to witness your heart outside of your own body.

As You

1. Your mind, not only fiercely intelligent but
wise,
Incredible.

2. Your heart, unimaginable compassion,
beautiful and authentic,
Pure.

3. Your humor and how wonderfully matched your
devilish wit meets mine,
Hell.

4. Your voice, in all its forms, how it
calms me, awakens me, comforts me, and
excites me,
Simultaneous.

5. Your spirituality and this constant
continuum of growth you chase,
Seek.

6. Your perspective, the way you see the
world, my favorite window,
Glimpse.

7. Your arms and how I feel wrapped inside
them,
Secure.

SUNFLOWER SHIN SPLINTS

8. Your body and blissfully responsive

nerve endings,

Sensation.

9. Your hands and how they perfectly research and
react to my body,
Titillating.

10. Your eyes, how deep they are, perfect for falling
into,

Wish

Seen

You see me,
You've always seen me.

Not what I could be,
Not some far-fetched fantasy,
Just me.

In all my chaotic glory,
You saw the storm,
And wished to feel the rain.

You saw the cracks,
And complimented my "golden joinery,"
My imperfect craftsmanship.

You didn't glaze over the dark,
You didn't ignore the deficiencies,
You didn't fabricate some beautiful ribbon,
To hold together the pieces of me,
Others would have thrown away.

You had no desire to manipulate,
The truth of me,
Into something more palatable,
More standard.

SUNFLOWER SHIN SPLINTS

You wished only to bask in my light,
Accompany me in my dark,
Push me towards growth,
And love the entirety of me.

Five of My Flaws and Why I Love Them

We are so accustomed in our culture to label our character attributes as assets or flaws. I believe there is an intrinsic self-judgment that precedes this practice. And for someone with my pessimistic leanings, where there is judgment, there can be an absence of love. I am easily my harshest critic and I feel that is true for so many of us. As a survivor of abuse and a woman focused on healing these traumas, I want my focus to be on love rather than judgment. I have found that there is beauty in the darkest parts of us, as well as the light. That there is space to accept these parts of myself and find usefulness to them. So here are five of my "flaws," how they are useful and why I love them.

1. I am idealistic and a hopeless romantic. This has left me vulnerable to only seeing the potential and entering unhealthy relationships, BUT it also allows me to find such beauty in even the smallest of things. It has

kept me soft even through all the harshness of life.

2. I am sarcastic and self-deprecating. No doubt a response created by trauma and low self-esteem, BUT it also means I can laugh during horrid times. And if used gently I can point out areas of myself that still need attention.

3. I have depression and suffer from suicidal ideation, BUT this pushes me to live a full life. I have made the decision to live and therefore I choose every day to chase happiness and fulfillment even harder.

4. I have anxiety, sometimes it can be crippling, BUT it forces me to live in the moment to function. And that simple act grants me a wonderful perspective of myself and my life.

5. My ego suffers from inflated imposter syndrome that can make me arrogant and argumentative, BUT it gives my pendulum a good starting spot to swing into appropriate confidence and eloquence.

I feel as though I have wasted so much time wrapped in a noose of self-hatred and its impossible-to-escape cycle. Held by this threadbare heirloom that only through self-flagellation can one achieve perfection. Somewhere along the path I discovered that it might be possible for more healing through acceptance rather than constant deprecation. Not every day, but more days than not I find myself loving this complex human.

Hopeful Romanticism

I want to fall in love with the universe. I want butterflies over sunsets and cotton candy skies.

I want goosebumps over nights full of stargazing.

I want involuntary chest expansion at the sight of shooting stars.

I want to crave her beauty, desire the sound of her songbirds as I do air.

I want to devote time to seeing more of her in all of her blissful seasons.

I want to find the beauty and graces in her most wild scenes.

I want to swoon from the power of her oceans.

I want to lust after the caress of her breeze across my cheek.

I want to be so enraptured by the universe that any lesser power has not a chance of diverting my attention.

With Myself in The Meadow

This shall pass, but what does that matter if I'm just right back here next year? It will just keep coming. There will be another break and god will fill that crack with more gold. What if I break so many times that my whole being is just gold? I become this perfect gleaming, broken, mended thing, glittering in the sun, bright as the beams themselves. Radiating light from all the places god has put my soul back together.

My thoughts constantly evolve with each transition, every moment signaling a shift in perspective. Until my trauma is a Monet and my present some cubism nonsense that only fellow aliens can recognize. The more authentic I become, the farther I am placed from the reality all the other earth dwellers exist in. Will this loneliness eventually make room for a gorgeous calm of contentment? When will I transcend from "by myself" to a position "with myself?" Will I recognize when this occurs? Will I even notice that I have arrived in the meadow, or will it simply grow up around me? One fragile sprout at a time slowly breaching the ashes at my feet. If that is the process, where do I exist now? Is this my future or my present? How many blades of perceived weeds are the buds of angelic bluebonnets in their first spring?

What if my perceived panic attacks aren't my body fighting its own existence but are growth spurts? Is my physical body dying to make space for the spiritual? What will I be after this break? One more glittering sliver across the surface of my being, to be presented to the next broken piece that I find.

I'm a crier now, but in the past, I had a catalyst compilation playlist when I needed to steam release. It was exclusively videos of soldiers' homecomings to their dogs.

Respite

Velvet indigo sky bookended by dueling mountain ranges of pine forest silhouettes. A forgotten mountain highway made romantic by a midsummer full moon and her stolen light.

Winding through mostly abandoned coal towns, air heavy with history and smog. The depressive stagnation of coal plumes is replaced by fog delicately draped across the foothills of the lower terrace as dawn begins to break. The horizon mirroring my brightening soul.

Every twist of the road brings renewed life to weary eyes as the New York border comes into view. Deep inhale at the awareness. Just like that, 21 hours drift away, I made it, I made it home.

Climb

We will be polished grit.
We will be smoothed river stones.
We will be real.

Imperfectly beautiful,
Impeccably crafted
By our struggles.

Thrivers amongst a forest of complacency,
We do not have the luxury of stagnation,
Our restless souls won't allow it.

We are cut from the cloth of warriors,
Not soldiers,
We do not settle for survival.

The hope that keeps us fighting is not merely
the next breath,
Not the uncertainty of the next sunrise.

Our goal is not a destination, nor
accomplishment.
We are the vining tendrils as they climb the
brick,
Not in search of the roofline,
but the sun.

P.S.

If you are reading this, you have successfully navigated through some of the darkest moments of my life and journeyed the sometimes-illusive path to the present. That is no small feat, if I do say so myself. Romantic violence, sexual assault, poverty, mental illness, and generational trauma, oh my. This collection is by no means an in-depth look at these topics, nor is it an unabridged explanation of the healing process. It is meant to be a glimpse, a snapshot of a full life lived, despite forces that have come to snuff out that light.

For me this journey continues to be nothing like what I would have expected, an ever-changing landscape with as many pitfalls as life-giving panoramic vistas.
The very moment I feel as though I'm getting my solid footing, the stone gives way. Sometimes to help me avoid a land clearing brush fire, and sometimes guides me to witnessing the sprouting result of new growth.

Many of these pieces I never wanted to write, let alone give off to the world for

mass consumption. I held to the belief that my
story was too unpleasant to share, while
simultaneously not being "that bad." A fun
little Tilt-a-whirl of delusion, party of one.
The truth I have come to realize is that my
story is just that, my story; and the fact that
my life up to now has been survived is pretty
spectacular. I wish that through these pages you
have been able to find hope, perspective, and
maybe connection. Until we meet again.

Imperfectly yours,

Siobhan Darling

SUNFLOWER SHIN SPLINTS

.